Patrick Ellrott

Black Identity in Toni Morrison's "The Bluest Eye"

GRIN Verlag

Bibliografische Information der Deutschen Nationalbibliothek:

Die Deutsche Bibliothek verzeichnet diese Publikation in der Deutschen Nationalbibliografie; detaillierte bibliografische Daten sind im Internet über http://dnb.d-nb.de/ abrufbar.

Imprint:

Druck und Bindung: Books on Demand GmbH, Norderstedt Germany
ISBN: 978-3-656-54032-8

This book at GRIN:

http://www.grin.com/en/e-book/263949/black-identity-in-toni-morrison-s-the-bluest-eye

Ellrott, Patrick

Black Identity in Toni Morrison's *The Bluest Eye*

Hausarbeit zur Lehrveranstaltung: Toni Morrison
Im WS 2008

table of contents page

Introduction

The purpose of this thesis is to show the destruction of identity in *The Bluest Eye*. In order to find out how far Toni Morrison digests her own experiences in her first piece of work, it is important to have a closer insight into her biography. First of all, I will provide the reader with some basic information about the author and genesis of the work in order to find out how far Toni Morrison dwells on her past. It is necessary to reflect on the underlying reasons why Toni Morrison started writing *The Bluest Eye*, as her motivation reveals the emotional attachment she has to her work. Hence, *The Bluest Eye* is introduced. The primer depicts the main aspects around the *Bluest Eye* and how it deals with identity formation and the tremendous problem with the context of beauty. Subsequently, I will give a definition of social identity to lay the foundation and back my argumentation. In this context, the concept of beauty plays a major role. I will illustrate the difficult situation of black people in a dominant white culture and how some black characters in *The Bluest Eye* are developed as a result of this. After that, I will present a sociological view of this problem and describe how Morrison's characters developed their identities by classifying them into categories. In my conclusion, I will discuss the main character's identities and highlight the differences between the MacTeers and the Breedloves.

2. Autobiographical influences

Morrison's biography reveals the importance of class identity and racial identity in the first 25 years of her life. For middle-class white America, blackness seems to be connected to poverty. The poorer one is, the blacker they appear. Therefore, Morrison welcomed the "black is beautiful"[1] and the Black Aesthetic Movement and started writing in 1965. The 1970s was an extremely politically active dacade during which time the Civil Rights Movement and the Women's Movement were in full blossom. "Morrison works in the space between a modernist desire for authentic identity and a postmodern understanding of the constructedness of all identity" (Duvall 18).

Morrison was born Chloe Anthony Wofford on the 18th of February 1931 in the Midwest, Lorain, Ohio. She was educated at Cornell University and Howard University. At first, she

---

[1] "The intensified black identity and the 'black is beautiful' attitude pushed light-skinned blacks from a position of advantage to one of disadvantage within the black community. The awakening of racial and ethnic identity allows people to be proud of their heritage and their distinct racial and ethinc group memberships" (Babad 146).

taught English and humanities at Texas Southern as well as Howard University. In 1960 she married the Jamaican architect Harold Morrison and gave birth to their two sons Slade and Ford, but separated four years after their marriage and got divorced subsequently.
Being born Chloe Anthony, Morrison explains her name change was due to problems of pronunciation at University, which seems a bit far-fetched, as there is a certain similarity to Claudia concerning the sound.
Toni Morrison states her book is not generally to be regarded as autobiographical: "People ask, 'Is your book autobiographical?' It is not, but it is, because of that process of reclamation." (Naylor 199). In another Interview with Bessie W. Jones and Audrey Vinson Toni Morrison admits that in writing she is re-doing the past (cf. Jones & Vinson 171). Furthermore, Ferguson describes Morrison's writing as a rediscovery, and even a reinscription of a part of Morrison's self which seems to be dead (cf. Ferguson 26). Nevertheless, the content of *The Bluest Eye* is based on personal experiences and sentiments:

> I used to love my company and then I didn't. And I realized the reason I didn't like my company was because there was nobody there to like. [...] all I needed was a slogan: 'Black is Beautiful'. It wasn't that easy being a little black girl in this country-it was rough. The psychological tricks you have to play in order to get through-and nobody said how it felt to be that. And you knew better. You knew inside better (Naylor 199).

In her first book Toni Morrison chose to use her hometown Lorain, Ohio for the setting:

> [...] [I] used literal descriptions of neighborhoods and changed the obvious things, the names of people, and mixed things all up, but the description of the house where we lived, the description of the streets, the lake, and all of that, is very much the way I remember Lorain, Ohio, [...] (Jones & Vinson 171).

Toni Morrison never lived in a black neighborhood in Lorain. There, black people were rare at that time. Thus, Morrison lived next door to white people and grew up with both, black and white people, just like Claudia and Frieda do. Another similarity is embodied in Frieda, Claudia's younger sister. Toni Morrison herself has an older sister, but their relationship is very different from the one portrayed in *The Bluest Eye*. Morrison admits that she was a cheery and clever girl who disagreed quite often and detested "white plastic celebrities of white culture". As a result, she hated all that concerned Shirley Temple (cf. Dowling 50).

Morrison's parents, Ramah Willis Wofford and George Wofford were among the first ones to migrate north because of the racial climate (cf. Jackson 87).

Moreover, Mr. MacTeer is a great deal like Morrison's own father, George Wofford, who worked in the shipyards, : " [...] could be very aggressive about people who troubled us-throwing people out and so on [...]" (Jones & Vinson 172). Her father once pushed a white man down the stairs. But his children were cared for properly and received his love. He always used to tell ghost stories to his children at night (cf. Dowling 50). Furthermore, her mother's unbreakable habit to moan about troublesome issues for days is taken up in the depiction of Mrs. MacTeer moaning about Pecola's thirst for milk for instance.

Even the leading motive originates from a conversation with a friend from her childhood:

> The conversation was about whether God existed; she said no and I said yes. She explained her reason for knowing that he did not: she had prayed every night for two years for blue eyes and didn't get them, and therefore he didn't exist. What I later recollected was that I looked at her and imagined her having them and thought how awful that would be if she had gotten her prayer answered. I always thought she was beautiful (Ruas 95).

Morrison herself is pretty light-skinned. As a result, her outward appearance is much closer to Maureen Peal than to Pecola. But in respect of class, Morrison was closer to Pecola. Furthermore, Morrison experienced her own family breakdown.

<u>3. Genesis of *The Bluest Eye*</u>

Morrison begins writing *The Bluest Eye* for the sake of bringing something to a writer's group in 1962:

> Then one day I didn't have anything to bring, so I wrote a little story about a black girl who wanted blue eyes. It was written hurriedly and probably not very well, but I read it and some liked it-I was 30 years old then so I wasn't a novice. Still, I thought it was finished; I'd written it, had an audience, so I put it aside (Watkins 44).

The divorce brought along a state of unhappiness, and that is when Toni Morrison started to change that short story into a novel. In doing so she wanted to give insights into the black point of view, which was neglected in most of the literature of the time: " [...] when I wrote *The Bluest Eye*, I was under the distinct impression, which was erroneous, that it was on me, you know, that nobody else was writing like that, nobody, and nobody was going to." (Naylor 212). She describes her motivation in an interview with Charles Ruas: "I was preoccupied with books by black people that approached the subject, but I always missed some intimacy -, some direction, some voice" (Ruas 96). Obviously, Morrison wrote that novel because she wanted to read it herself: "My audience is always the people in the book I'm writing at the time. I don't think of an external audience" (Tate 161).

4. *The Bluest Eye*

Ferguson describes *The Bluest Eye* as a post-Civil Rights Movement work as it deals with a variety of subjects of class during that era. But it is not about class primarily, it is about "[...] distorted, contradictory self-perceptions imposed upon black people by the dominant white culture." (Ferguson 23).[2]

One main aspect concerns white physical beauty standards and its tremendous impact on black people who are not able to conform to them: "Within the novel Morrison demonstrates that even with the best intentions, people hurt each other when they are chained to circumstances of poverty and low social status" (McKay 138). The story is representative for most people living up North around 1940: "[...] *The Bluest Eye* (1970), encouraged many of us to speak for the first time about the enormous damage to the psyche that results from trying to adopt an alien standard of beauty (Wilson 129). Morrison did: "[...] write about a girl who wanted blue eyes and the horror of having that wish fulfilled; and also about the whole business of what physical beauty and the pain of that yearning and wanting to be somebody else [...]" (Ruas 95). On the very first page she explains what happened. Then, she explains *how* and what comes from the inability to express love. In the end the first-person narrator Claudia realizes that: "The damage was done total. She spent her days, her tendril, sap-green days, walking up and down, her head jerking to the beat of a drummer so distant only she could hear" (Morrison 162).

Duvall states that "Morrison's first four novels [including *The Bluest Eye*], which overtly represent identity formation, serve as the writer's reflections on the fictions of identity" (Duvall 10).

---

[2] "The majority culture aims at 'acculturating' the minority groups, demanding conformity to its norms and standards – not only through obedience to the law but through the internalization of its values and ways of life as well." (Babad 156).

Ferguson explored Morrison's notion of identity, as a process concerning relationship including social, familial, racial and psychological aspects. An identity crisis originates from the lack of a positive self-image because of interactions with a group. Pecola goes mad in the end because of the dominant white culture and a lack of people to provide her with what she needs to develop a healthy identity.

5. Primer

The Dick-and Jane primer is taken from a traditional American children's reading book and presents the white stereotypes; social ideals as it describes a typical white American nuclear middle-class family, which was the way life was presented to black people:

> Here is the House. It is green and white. It has a red door. It is very pretty. Here is the family Mother, Father, Dick and Jane live in the green-and-white house. They are very happy. See Jane. She has a red dress. She wants to play. Who will play with Jane? See the cat. It goes meow-meow. Come and play. Who will play with Jane? The kitten will not play. See Mother. Mother is very nice. Mother, will you play with Jane? Mother laughs. Laugh, Mother laugh. See Father. He is big and strong. [...] (Morrison 1).

To Jane's house belong a cat, a nice mother, a big and strong father and a dog. Though none of them will play with Jane in her nice dress, she finally finds a friend for a good game. This family is happy and everything seems to be alright. When it is repeated, first the punctuation, then the capitals and in the end the spaces between the words are omitted. Toni Morrison makes use of that primer in order to emphasize "the way life was presented to black people. As the novel proceeded I wanted that primer version broken up and confused, which explains the typographical running together of the words" (LeClair 127). Chikwenye Okonjo Ogunemi considers the three paragraphs as a representation of three families being introduced in *The Bluest Eye*: "Geraldine's family, which is the closest to the ideal family of the primer, the MacTeers, and finally the Breedloves, who are at the bottom of the social hierarchy"(O'Reilly 49). Furthermore, he suggests that the primer constitutes Morrison's criticism of the white majority's nonreflective way of dealing and the operational application of those textbooks in school. Learning how to read is strongly connected to taking on standard values. This primers function was to teach how to learn to read, but it also shows how children also internalize the values posed in the text.

Morrison's complex family structures contradict the image of the white patriarchal nuclear family and therefore, the latter cannot serve as a template for analyzing African American families. It is striking to see that all of the depicted characters live in matriarchal households.

6. A definition of social identity

With regard to social psychology, people start to acquire a social identity.
Basically, an identity characterizes an individual person in distinguishing his or her characteristics from other people's. Identity formation starts early in life and depends on cultural demands and personal capacity. Decisions and virtues of others play an important role in this context. Social Identity; a self-definition that helps to evaluate oneself. This includes many unique characteristics like a name and self-concept as well as characteristics we share with others like gender, vocation, political and ideological attitudes and other specific attitudes. In short social identity is: "A person's definition of who he or she is, including personal attributes and attributes shared with others, such as gender and race" (Baron & Byrne 161).

7. Unique identity: the self

For each person the self is the center of the world. Self-identity or self-concept is basically the result of what we have learned from other people starting with parents and other immediate family members. At a later time, the self-identity gets influenced by people beyond the family. In summary, it can be said, that: "One's self-identity, is a basic schema consisting of an organized collection of beliefs and attitudes about oneself" (Baron &Byrne 162).

8. Concept of beauty and it's consequences

Shirley Jane Temple, born in 1928 was the 1930s child film star and America's littlest minstrel. She achieved iconic status and was loved throughout America. Her golden locks, blue eyes and pale skin were generally seen as an image of perfection. At the age of twelve years she had made 24 feature films already. Claudia resisted this ideal of beauty:

> Frieda and she [Pecola] had a loving conversation about how cu-ute Shirley Temple was. I couldn't join them in their adoration because I hated Shirley. Not because she

> was cute, but because she danced with Bojangles, who was *my* friend, *my* uncle, *my* daddy, and who ought to have been soft-shoeing it and chuckling with me (Morrison 13).

At a first glance Claudia seems to admit envy. Bojangles, Bill Robinson, was a black actor famous for his tap-dance. He was the first African-American male to appear on film dancing with a white girl – Shirley Temple. But then Claudia goes on:

> Younger than both Frieda and Pecola, I had not yet arrived at the turning point in the development of my psyche which would allow me to love her. What I felt at that time was unsullied hatred. But before that I had felt a stranger, more frightening thing than hatred for all the Shirley Temples of the world. (Morrison 13)

In her early childhood Claudia feels alienated from her community. She does not understand why all the people surrounding her felt, that being blue-eyed and blond was beautiful. Therefore, she does not appreciate her gift for Christmas – a blue-eyed baby doll, pretty similar in appearance to Shirley Temple. First of all, she is not interested in pretending motherhood, and second, Claudia does not find the doll comfortable because it is made from hard plastic. She is interested in only one thing:

> [...] to dismember it. To see of what it was made, to discover the dearness, to find the beauty, the desirability that had escaped me, but apparently only me. Adults, older girls, shops, magazines, newspapers, window signs - all the world had agreed that a blue-eyed, yellow-haired, pink skinned doll was what every girl child treasured. (Morrison 14)

In 1951 Kenneth and Mamie Clark developed a doll test. Clark invited 16 black children to choose one from identical brown and white colored dolls. The result was upsetting. Ten of the girls preferred the white doll. Seven of them pointed to the white doll when they were asked to choose the one which is the most like themselves and eleven of those girls referred to the black dolls as "bad" (cf. Douglas 149).

Thus, Claudia cannot really understand why Maureen Peal, a near white, green eyed classmate:

> [...] enchanted the entire school. When teachers called on her, they smiled encouragingly. Black Boys didn't trip her in the halls; white boys didn't stone her, white girls didn't suck their teeth when she was assigned to be their work partners; black girls stepped aside when she wanted to use the sink in the girls' toilet, and their

eyes genuflected under sliding lids. She never had to search for anybody to eat with in the cafeteria [...] (Morrison 48).

Unlike Claudia, Clark's students were not able to move from preference to identification unperturbed. Some of the children broke down when they were asked to make self-identifications (cf. Douglas 150). Those children must identify with what they reject. This leads to a: "fundamental conflict at the very foundations of the ego structure" (Douglas 150).

9. Blackness opposed to Whiteness

In order to understand the position of black people around 1940, it is important to have a closer look at how Blackness was represented back at that time. The popular minstrel show was an excellent example for black performances demonstrating the complex relationship between white and black people. White Americans countered the expanding black population with: "[...] part fear, part anxiety, part desire[...]" (Hébert 184). Therefore, blackness in a sense of the minstrel show is defined by white people representing black men as non-human and harmless curiosities and has its origins in Europe: "[...] there are no 'niggers' outside of a European-centered paradigm" (Hébert 185). Back in medieval Europe, 'pickaninnies'[3] were depicted as imps and devils, who were dangerous for white people. The minstrel show accentuated black peculiarities and inferiority as it represented black people as beings who had wool instead of hair, eyes sticking out, flat and broad-nose, dangling lips and enormous feet.

Nevertheless, these performances influenced the self-perception of many people of African descent, unfortunately.

Toni Morrison introduces Whiteness as an antagonism to Blackness. Affected by those fatal impressions, most of the characters in The Bluest Eye are deracinated from their community's original blackness: "By reconstructing herself in the white image centered in Western culture as human, Pecola performs, in some sense, her own black version of a white-faced -black performance" (Hébert 193). Toni Morrison moves from the big picture into more specific detail. America's erasure of its desire for black culture. Pecola wants to erase visible traits of race; she wants to disappear (cf. Morrison 34). Realizing her eyes will

[3] Derogatory expression for small black children.

not go, she wants to turn them blue in order to be different; see the world differently, become somebody else.

Geraldine and Maureen are "[...] of a type of people who are losing a cultural identity that is rightfully theirs because of their racial ancestry" (Douglas 141). Those people come from "Mobile", "Aiken", "Newport News", "Marietta" or "Meridian" and do "not sweat in their armpits nor between [their] thighs, who smelled of wood and vanilla, and who had made soufflés in the Home Economics Department [...]" (Morrison 67). Morrison describes "them" as "thin brown girls" who live in "quiet black neighborhoods" where "everybody is gainfully employed"; are rich enough to have a refrigerator, are "narrow, tall, and still" (cf. Morrison 64). They learn how to behave with regard to white standards and keep funkiness under for a lifetime. All of ther life they will never be completely accepted by society even though they worry about their straightened hair will turn into its original form: "the line between colored and nigger was not always clear; subtle and telltale signs threatened to erode it, and the watch had to be constant" (Morrison 68). They try to conform to white cultural normativity. For Geraldine Whiteness it is not a question of skin color. Geraldine is colored and does not like her son to play with "niggers": "She had explained to him the difference between colored people and niggers. They were easily identifiable. Colored people were neat and quiet; niggers were dirty and loud" (Morrison 67). So Geraldine makes her son wear: "white shirts and blue trousers, his hair was cut as close to his scalp as possible to avoid any suggestion of wool" (Morrison 67).

Douglas concludes: "Geraldine can't change her race, but she can try to change her culture, and this process is described as loss rather than gain or transformation" (Douglas 144).

10. Black identity

With regard to racial identity development diverse terminology was used. Quite a lot of people get the term wrong and consider that Black or White constitute a feature for *racial identity*, but actually the term "[...] refers to a sense of group or collective identity based on one's *perception* that he or she shares a common racial heritage with a particular racial group" (Helms 3). In fact, it takes a combination of physical characters, of genetic origin to belong to a sub-group. Race and ethnicity are not to be used synonymously, as ethnicity is not biologically defined. As a result, " [...] members of different racial groups could belong to the same ethnic group" (Helms 4).

Black racial identity theories try to explain distinct ways "in which Blacks can identify (or not identify) with other Blacks [...]" (Helms 5). There are four categories to stick to: Whites primarily, Blacks primarily, both or neither. Therefore, one may have a mono-racial, a bi-racial or a marginal ascribed identity. A black person who is oriented by a white reference-group conceives the own racial-group membership to be unsuitable to his or her personal living conditions and wants to become a member of the white society by means of adopting white standards (cf. Helms 6).

Helms states that: "[...] three components - personal identity, reference-group orientation, and ascribed identity-undoubtedly interact with each other" (Helms 6).

Consequently, if one racial group is associated with negative stereotypes, it is more than likely that a racial group associated with positive stereotypes is chosen for both reference group and source of ascribed identity[4]. As a result, Helms concludes: [...] such identifications become problematic to the extent that they require denial or distortions of oneself and/or the racial group(s) from which one descends" (Helms 6).

10.1 Stages of identity development

One of the two mayor black racial identity theoretical strands is called "NRID" which stands for "Nigrescene or racial identity development". In the context of NRID, theorists tried to find out what it takes for the development of a healthy black identity. They assumed overidentification with white standards "was a psychologically unhealthy resolution of the identity issues resulting from one's need to survive in a racist culture" (Helms 17). As a result, stage models moving from the least healthy, white-determined stages of identity, to most healthy, self-defined racial supremacy. Each of the four or five stages, respectively, brings along different behaviors, feelings and thoughts for the individual person. It is possible to progress from the least developed stage to the most developed.

The *Preencounter* stage is defined by the absence of a self-concept. The dominant white culture is idealized and the black world view is devalued. The black person "must find some way to separate himself or herself from the devalued reference group in order to minimize the psychological discomfort that arises when one's cognitions are incompatible" (Helms 20). There are two kinds of Preencounter, active or passive. Often the passive kind is

[4] "Sociologists speak of ‚ascribed status' as that confirmed by social characteristics, primarily race, religion, and ethnicity, acquired at birth and usually retained by the individual for better or worse throughout life" (Babad 143).

thought to be connected to a healthier personal identity than the active kind. In active Preencounter, Blacks and black culture is degraded and a separation from personal identity takes place. Everything that does conform to white standard is perceived as pleasing. "Thus, it is not unusual to hear 'successful' Blacks argue that they reject other Blacks as a reference group because their values or behaviors are so different" (Helms 22). It is believed that persons in the active kind of the Preencounter stage tend to have low self-esteem, poor self-concept, high anxiety and depression.

Passive Preencounter persons think that personal effort is connected to admittance into white culture. These people are hard to discern, because they seem to be fairly assimilated to the dominant white society.

In short, the Preencounter person comes to perceive that he or she does not really 'fit' into either group unconditionally. The conscious acknowledgement of alienation initiates her or his movement into Encounter stage" (Helms 24).

At "Encounter" stage a person realizes that it is impossible for him or her to enter the white world and become a fully acknowledged member. After having abandoned the Preencounter identity the individual is confronted with "feelings including confusion, hopelessness, anxiety, depression, and eventually anger and euphoria" (Helms 25). If you will reach this stage, it represents taking the first step towards a Black ascribed identity. Still, the person is identity-less.

The next phase is divided into "Immersion" and "Emersion". In Immersion a person perceives the black world to be highly seductive and acts the way in which he expects authentic "blackish" people will act. Typically, such persons idealize black standards and African heritage and are angry at Whites because of Slavery. For Emersion it takes withdrawal into a black community, which results in a non-stereotypic black perspective. By finding out what black culture is about, one gets more independent from other opinions: "Total acceptance as defined by others is no longer necessary for the person to feel self-worth, and he or she begins to sort out the strengths and weaknesses of Black culture and being Black" (Helms 28) whereas Whiteness is denigrated.

During the "Internalization" phase a positive personally relevant Black identity gets internalized and Blacks finally turn into the primary reference group a person belongs to. The phase includes personal strength and the rejection of racism or even social activism.

10.2 [Black] identity in *The Bluest Eye*

Unlike Pecola, Claudia's concept of beauty is not that much influenced by the dominant society:

> "Guileless and without vanity, we [Frieda and Claudia] were still in love with ourselves then. We felt comfortable in our skins, enjoyed the news that our senses released to us, admired our dirt, cultivated our scars and could not comprehend this unworthiness" (Morrison 57).

Claudia begins the "Autumn" narrative with encountering Rosemary Villanucci, a white, wealthy neighbor:

> Rosemary Villanucci, our next-door friend who lives above her father's café, sits in a 1939 Buick eating bread and butter. She rolls down the window to tell my sister Frieda and me that we can't come in. We stare at her, wanting her bread, but more than that, wanting to poke the arrogance out of her eyes and smash the pride of ownership that curls her chewing mouth. When she comes out of the car we will beat her up , make red marks on her white skin [...]. [...] that our own pride must be asserted [...] (Morrison 5).

Obviously, in this situation Claudia and Frieda are confused and do not know what to do. Firstly, they want to have what Rosemary has (buttered bread). Secondly, they wish to enter Rosemary's world and thirdly, they want to " [...] force her to become like themselves" (Ferguson 36).

We do not learn a lot about Mr. and Mrs. MacTeer. But what we do know is that they care for their children. This is why Mr. MacTeer put Mr. Henry outdoors, when he tries to assault Frieda (cf. Morrison 76). When Claudia catches a cough, after a trip to collect coal, her mother tucks her in. After a while Claudia throws up and observes her puke with admiration: "The puke swaddles down the pillow onto the sheet - green-gray, with flecks of orange. It moves like the insides of an uncooked egg. Stubbornly clinging to its own mass, refusing to break up and be removed. How, I wonder, can it be so neat and nasty at the same time?" (Morrison 6). Claudia regards herself – spirit and body as an entity. Even her puke is conceived as attractive on the one hand and awful on the other hand. Therefore, Claudia's puke: "[...] is so much a part of her and her present condition that it is identified with herself and addressed as if it were herself" (Ferguson 32). When Mrs. MacTeer comes in to wipe up the puke, she starts yelling. But Claudia realizes that: "She is not talking to me.

She is talking to the puke, but she is calling it my name: Claudia" (Morrison 6f.) Even if Mrs. MacTeer seems to be rude, Claudia realizes her mother's love and so she concludes: "So when I think of autumn, I think of somebody with hands who does not want me to die" (Morrison 7).

"I could smell it [Love] – taste it – sweet, musty, with an edge of wintergreen in its base – everywhere in that house" (Morrison 7). Therefore, Claudia has got the possibility to withdraw into the Black community, get actively protected and for all the roughness that her mother oftentimes shows, receive love.

Moreover, Claudia's disdainfulness of white baby dolls shows healthy self-esteem. However, later on Claudia admits she learns to love Shirley Temple and does not deny white standards. In spite of her admitting she likes Shirley Temple, Claudia is sufficiently reassured of her-self, race and community and for insufficient information she is probably in the Emersion stage.

Pecola's parents Pauline and Cholly Breedlove have a bad marriage. They are a family by name only. Cholly and Pauline came north for opportunities[5], representing 6 million black people during "The Great Migration".

Pauline, began to feel lonely and alienated. As a result she sought refuge into the white world and learned a lot about white stereotypes and prejudices[6] which: "[...] are not necessarily based on people's first-hand experiences with members of stereotyped groups. They may be learned from others or from the mass media" (Babad 75). Pauline finds distraction by going to the movies where she is convinced that she is ugly[7], because what is defined as pretty means having blonde hair and blue eyes. By those:" [...] unimaginative, perfected images of the romantic cinema" (Ferguson 34) Pauline learned that if you were a white woman with blond hair and blue eyes, equality, happiness and worthiness were for sure. Bit by bit Pauline became a conformist and tried to enter a society she would never belong to: "*The Bluest Eye* serves to emphasize the inappropriateness of this ideal for black families and reminds us of the inevitable feelings of inferiority that come with not achieving

---

[5] Morrison's parents migrated from Georgia and Alabama ans settled in Lorain, Ohio, west of Cleveland.

[6] "'Prejudice' is a special category of stereotypes, characterized by a negative emotional tone and a hostileand aggressive nature. While stereotypes are mechanisms of cognitively organizing and simplifying the complexity of the social environment, prejudices are statements of superiority, hateful attitudes that pave the way for the practice of discrimination in the form of racism, sexism, nationalism, religious fanatism, and the like" (Babad 75)

[7] „Once stereotypes are held, [...] people seek instances that will confirm them. They attend selectively and seek confirming information and at the same time are highlyresistant to disconfirming information" (Babad 83)

what is presented as the ideal and normal way of being" (O'Reilly 48). By giving in to the dominant society, she accepted that she was ugly in opposition to the White's dearness: "Although their poverty was traditional and stultifying, it was not unique. But their ugliness was unique. No one could have convinced them that they were not relentlessly and aggressively ugly" (Morrison 28). Being not able to conform her house and family to white (and destructive standards) her life: "were like the afterthoughts one has just before sleep, the early-morning and late-evening edges of her day, the dark edges that made the daily life with the Fishers lighter, more delicate, more lovely" (Morrison 99).

Being influenced by what is presented in the cinema, Pauline developed a peculiar imagination of Pecola, when she was pregnant:

> Anyways, the baby come. Big old healthy thing. She looked different from what I thought. Reckon I talked to it so much before I conjured up a mind's eye view of it. So when I seed it, it was like looking at a picture of your mama when she was a girl. [...] A right smart baby she was. I used to like to watch her (Morrison 97).

In the end of this remark she becomes pretty expressional: "But I knowed she was ugly. Head full of pretty hair, but Lord she was ugly" (Morrison 98). On the one hand, Pauline is fascinated and attracted by little Pecola but on the other hand she feels repulsion. O'Reilly believes: "The child imagined in the womb is light skinned, fine featured [...] (O'Reilly 53). Even though Pauline gives the doctor contra when he explains to his students that black women do not feel any pain when giving birth, her self-esteem is reduced by her experiences at work and in the cinema, where she is regarded as unimportant and undesirable as a person. Alluding to a photo of her mother when she was still a baby, Pauline makes clear that it is necessary to love her own self if she was to love Pecola. Therefore, it is understandable that she perceives her own daughter as ugly.

Pauline herself feels denunciated by the society. She only feels accepted and tolerated when serving the Fishers: "The creditors and service people who humiliated her when she went to them on her own behalf respected, were even intimidated by her, when she spoke for the Fishers'" (Morrison 99). She even has a Nickname at the Fishers', feels comfortable, respected and loved in this surrounding. Having inhaled those ideals of beauty: "She was never able, after her education in the movies, to look at a face and not assign it some category in the scale of absolute beauty, and the scale was one she absorbed in full from the silverscreen" (Morison 95).

For Pauline, who is in the active kind of the Preencounter stage, the least healthy identity stage: "disconnection occurs as a result of migration and assimilation [...]" (O'Reilly 58).

Cholly Breedlove was rejected himself by his parents. His father ran away the day he was born and his mother disposed of him when he was three years old. After Aunt Jimmy, who took care of him, dies, he gets humiliated by white people. Being traumatized he seeks refuge with his father but again he faces rejection. The destruction of his self is complete:

> Finding the deepest shadow under the pier, he crouched in it, behind one of the posts. He remained knotted there in foetal position, paralyzed, his fists covering his eyes, for a long time. No sound, no sight, only darkness and hest and the press of his knuckles on his eyelids (Morrison 124).

His only image of a father figure is one who brings pain.

Harbourless, Cholly finds that even in his black community and family he cannot find shelter. The lack of his Family and community as a boy influenced the way he was as a man.

By raping his daughter his search for himself ends in destruction of himself. Emphasizing this in burning down the flat, he gives himself up. For Cholly, racial identity is not an issue. He spent his life searching for role models and orientation.

O'Reilly concludes: "Unable to love themselves, Cholly and Pauline cannot love their children because they are made from them and so are reflections of them" (O'Reilly 53).

Starting with the title of the novel, *The Bluest Eye* is ambiguous as "Eye" is a homophone for "I". In spite of spending hours in front of a mirror in order to discover her ugliness and not finding it Pecola is convinced that she can not put up with others. As early as she was given her name it was decided she would have to suffer from her blackness. Ferguson describes Pecola as "[...] a receptacle for whiteness [...] (Ferguson 37), as she drinks overmuch white milk from a Shirley Temple mug and favors *Mary Jane* candies because she admires her blue eyes, blond hair and white skin. Although she realizes that there is something wrong with Mary Jane due to her fractious and harmful eyes: "[...] to Pecola they are simply pretty. She eats the candy, and its sweetness is good" (Morrison 38). An illusionary identification takes place: "To eat the candy is somehow to eat the eyes, eat Mary Jane. Be Mary Jane. Three pennies had brought her nine lovely orgasms with Mary Jane" (Morrison 38). She feels rejected by her mother and father and therefore wishes to be different; she thinks: "If she looked different, beautiful, maybe Cholly would be different, and Mrs. Breedlove too. Maybe they'd say, 'Why, look at pretty-eyed Pecola. We mustn't do bad things in front of those pretty eyes' (Morrison 34).

Pecola's wish for blue eyes illustrates self-loathing. Initially, it is the wish to disappear when she witnesses a conflict between her mother, father and brother. She prays:

> "Please, God," she whispered into the palm of her hand. "Please make me disappear." She squeezed her eyes shut. Little parts of her body faded away. Now slowly, now with a rush. Slowly again. [...] Only her tight, tight eyes were left. They were always left (Morrison 33).

Another way to interpret Pecola's longing for milk is actually her longing for motherly love, as the only things she receives is lessons in what is to fear. The distanced relation between mother and daughter is emphasized by Pecola calling her mother Mrs. Breedlove. In the Fishers' kitchen she gets chased away by her mother and accepts with less resistance that she is not the desired and loved child of her mother. For a little girl, the love of her mother is the most important love she can receive. As a result, her: "[...] disconnection arises from a lack of maternal nurturance" (O'Reilly 58). With regard to her father Cholly she can never expect any guidance or affirmation. Her search for identity results from her acute shortage of love and is defined by her strong desire to be loved. Mr. Yacowbski represents society's attitudes toward black people by treating Pecola as if she was invisible: "How can a fifty-two year old white immigrant storekeeper [...] see a little black girl? (Morrison 36). Encounters with Mr. Yacowbski and Geraldine assure her that she really is a "nasty" little girl. After being raped by her father, she finds no one to talk to; Pecola can only talk to herself. After Pecola's wish to have blue eyes gets fulfilled, she invents a friend to negate her own self-less and invisible existence. She chooses a split identity in order to survive and puts her exclusion from society in terms she can comprehend. Just like her mother, Pecola is in the active kind of the Preencounter stage, minimizing the psychological discomfort arising from incompatible cognitions.

11. Conclusion

With regard to the title of this thesis, I would like to quote Duvall: "[...] the light-skinned, middle-class Maureen and Geraldine are demonized, and if the Breedloves fall victim to a culturally scripted racial self-loathing, the working-class MacTeer family nevertheless embodies the African-American ideal" (Duvall 21).

The Breedloves finished with different results: while Pecola is separated from society but content, Cholly is separated and unsatisfied. But Pauline is the only one who chooses an identity (a white one) to be content with.

Babad states: "It is ironic that the best strategy for maintaining cultural uniqueness and a distinct socio-identity is to remain segregated from the majority culture" (Babad 157).

It seems that Morrison wants to show neither the nuclear family, as presented in the primer, nor another concept for the family that can serve as a model for black families at that time. Instead, she shows the complexity of the African American family which is ruled by a complex history and heritage. Moreover, the MacTeers live under the same conditions as the Breedloves do. But the MacTeers do not collapse. Consequently, there must be a reason for this instability of the Breedloves. O'Reilly states Pauline's liability to beauty and romance remain inherent to her artistic sensibilities. Besides her preference to arrange things: "She missed-without knowing what she missed-paints and crayons" (Morrison 87). Whilst still being connected to her family and black community, she especially remembers colors: "My whole dress was messed with purple, and it never did wash out..." (Morrison 90).

She uses colors for descriptive purposes:

> I begin to feel those little bits of color floating up into me-deep in me. That streak of green from the june-bug light, the purple from the berries trickling along my thighs, Mama's lemonade yellow runs sweet in me. Then I feel like I'm laughing between my legs, and the laughing gets all mixed up with the colors [...]. And it be rainbow all inside (Morrison 102).

As soon as she goes north with Cholly and is apart from her black community she gets lonely: "It was hard to get to know folks up here, I missed my people" (Morrison 91). Pauline experiences mockery because she does not straighten her hair and the rainbow inside her fades away. Revealingly, she ends her monologue: "Only thing I miss sometimes is that rainbow. But like I say, I don't recollect it much anymore (Morrison 102).

Consequently, Pauline withdraws from her family. Morrison intended to show how vulnerable children are, especially black girls and how much they need support from both their family and community. While Mr. MacTeer protects his children from sexual infringements, Cholly himself rapes his daughter. In the end, even Pecola is not given any credibility and this is what constitutes Morrison's central statement in *The Bluest Eye*: a healthy identity is not destroyed due to social standards, but due to a lack of a loving and caring family.

12. Bibliography

Morrison, Toni. *The Bluest Eye*. London: Vintage, 1999.

Helms, Janet E, ed. *Black and White Racial Identity: Theory, Research and Practice.* New York: Greenwood Press, 1990.

Baron, Robert A., und Donn Byrne. *Social Psychology*. Boston [u.a.]: Allyn and Bacon, [10]2003.

Babad, Elisha Y., Max Birnbaum, und Kenneth D. Benne. *The Social Self: Group Influences on Personal Identity*. Beverly Hills: Sage, 1983.

Dowling, Colette. "The Song of Toni Morrison". *Conversations with Toni Morrison.* Hrsg. Danielle Taylor-Guthrie. Jackson: University Press of Mississippi, [6]2001. 48-59.

Duvall, John N. *The Identifying Fictions of Toni Morrison: Modernist Athenticity and Postmodern Blackness*. New York [u.a.]: Palgrave, 2000.

Fergusson, Rebecca H. *Rewriting Black Identities: Transition and Exchange in the Novels of Toni Morrison*. Bruxelles [u.a.]: Lang, 2007.

Hébert, Kimberly G. "Acting the Nigger: Topsy, Shirley Temple, and Toni Morrison's Pecola". *Approaches to Teaching Stowe's Uncle Tom's Cabin.* Hrsg. Elizabeth Ammons und Susan Belasco. New York: Modern Language Association of America, 2000.

Heinert, Jennifer L. J. *Narrative Conventions and Race in the Novels of Toni Morrison.* New York [u.a.]: Routledge, 2009.

Jackson, Tommie L. *"High-Topped Shoes"and Other Signifiers of Race, Class, Gender, and Ethnicity in Selected Fiction by William Faulkner and Toni Morrison*. Lanham [u.a.]: Univ. Press of America, 2006.

Jones, Bessie W. und Audrey Vinson. "An Interview with Toni Morrison". *Conversations with Toni Morrison.* Hrsg. Danielle Taylor-Guthrie. Jackson: University Press of Mississippi, [6]2001. 171-187.

LeClair, Thomas. "The Language Must Not Sweat: A Conversation with Toni Morrison". *Conversations with Toni Morrison.* Hrsg. Danielle Taylor-Guthrie. Jackson: University Press of Mississippi, [6]2001. 119-128.f

McKay, Nellie. "An Interview with Toni Morrison". *Conversations with Toni Morrison.* Hrsg. Danielle Taylor-Guthrie. Jackson: University Press of Mississippi, [6]2001. 138-155.

Morrison, Toni und Carolyn C. Denard, ed. W*hat Moves at the Margin.* Jackson, Miss.: Univ. Press of Mississippi, 2008.

Naylor, Gloria. "A Conversation: Gloria Naylor and Toni Morrison". *Conversations with Toni Morrison.* Hrsg. Danielle Taylor-Guthrie. Jackson: University Press of Mississippi, [6]2001. 188-217.

O'Reilly, Andrea. *Toni Morrison and Motherhood: A Politics of the Heart.* Albany: State Univ. of New York Press, 2004.

Ruas, Charles. "Toni Morrison". *Conversations with Toni Morrison.* Hrsg. Danielle Taylor-Guthrie. Jackson: University Press of Mississippi, [6]2001. 93-118.

Tate, Claudia. "Toni Morrison". *Conversations with Toni Morrison.* Hrsg. Danielle Taylor-Guthrie. Jackson: University Press of Mississippi, [6]2001. 156-170.

Watkins, Mel. "Talk with Toni Morrison". *Conversations with Toni Morrison.* Hrsg. Danielle Taylor-Guthrie. Jackson: University Press of Mississippi, [6]2001. 43-47.

Wilson, Judith. "A Conversation with Toni Morrison". *Conversations with Toni Morrison.* Hrsg. Danielle Taylor-Guthrie. Jackson: University Press of Mississippi, [6]2001. 129-137.

CPSIA information can be obtained at www.ICGtesting.com
Printed in the USA
LVOW11s0402250116

472124LV00005B/203/P